CONTENTS

Cover photo: Neil Zlozower/Atlasicons.com

ISBN 978-1-4950-0773-6

HAL•LEONARD®
CORPORATION
7777 W. BLUEMOUND RD. P.O. BOX 13819 MILWAUKEE, WI 53213

Visit Hal Leonard Online at
www.halleonard.com

Angel of Death

Words and Music by Jeff Hanneman

Slightly faster ♩ = 210

1.

2.

Verse

1. Ausch - witz, the meaning of pain, __ the way that I want __ you to die. __

Slow death, im - mense de - cay, __ show-ers that cleanse __ you of your life. Forced in like cat - tle, you run, stripped of your life's worth. Hu - man mice for the an - gel of death. Four hun - dred thou - sand more to die.

Chorus

3

Chorus

Strapped down, scream - ing out to die.

An - gel of death.

Mon - arch to the king - dom of the dead.

In - fa - mous butch - er,

an - gel of death!

Interlude
Slower ♩ = 183

5

Verse

3. Pumped with flu - id ___ in - side your brain.

Pres - sure in your skull be - gins push - ing through your eyes. Burn - ing flesh drips a - way.

Test of heat burns your skin. Your mind starts to boil. Frig - id cold

cracks your limbs. How long can you last in this fro - zen wa - ter bur - i - al?

Sewn to - geth - er, ___ join - ing heads. Just a mat - ter of time till you

rip your - selves a - part. Mil - lions laid out in their ___ crowd - ed

tombs. Sick - 'ning ways ___ to a -

chieve the Hol - o - caust.

Ran - cid   an - gel of   death   fly - ing

Interlude

Guitar Solo
Faster ♩ = 230

Slower ♩ = 210

Chorus

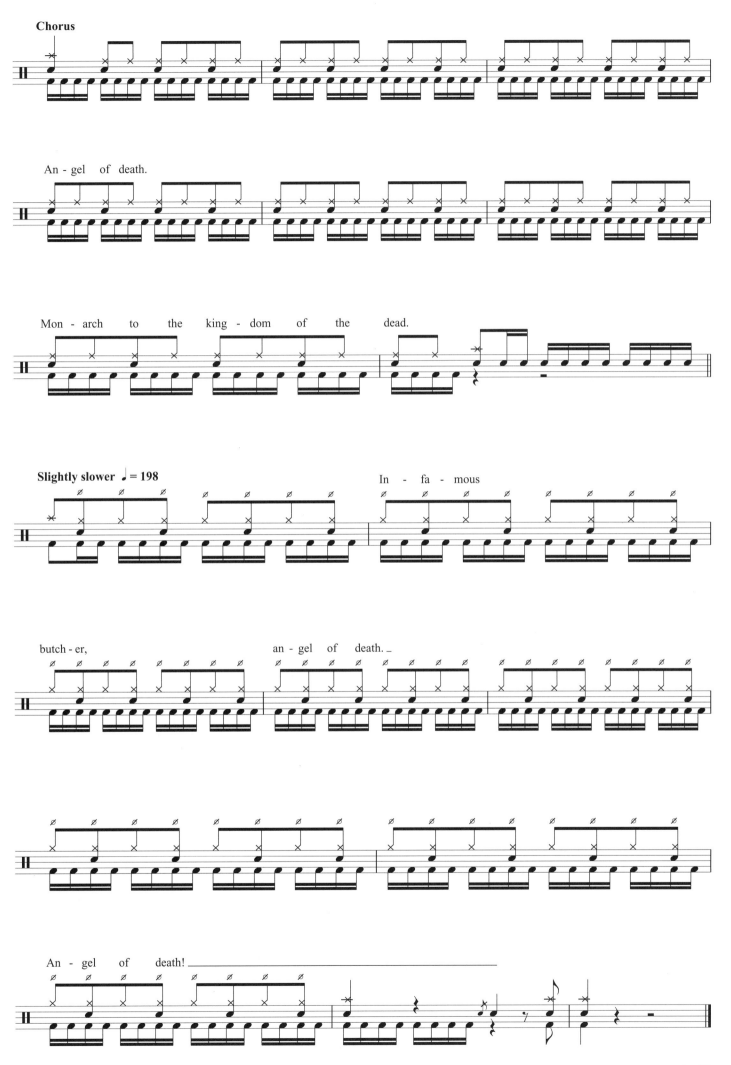

An - gel of death.

Mon - arch to the king - dom of the dead.

Slightly slower ♩ = 198

In - fa - mous

butch - er, an - gel of death.

An - gel of death!

Piece by Piece

Words and Music by Kerry King

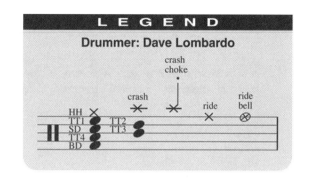

Outro-Chorus

Additional Lyrics

2. Bones and blood lie on the ground.
   Rotten limbs lie dead.
   Decapitated bodies found.
   On my wall, your head.

Pre-Chorus On your trail, I close the gap.
   One more life that soon won't be.
   No emotion, flesh is all I need.

Dead Skin Mask

Words and Music by Jeff Hanneman and Tom Araya

Intro
Moderately ♩ = 114

How I've waited for you to come. *I've been here all alone.*

Now that you've arrived, *please stay awhile,*

and I promise I won't keep you long. *I'll keep you forever.*

Verse
Slightly slower ♩ = 108

1. Graze the skin ___ with ___ my ___

___ fin - ger - tips. ___ The brush of dead, cold ___ flesh, ___ ap-pease ___ the means. ___

Pro - vok-ing im-ag-es, del - i -cate fea-tures so smooth, __ a pleas-ant fra-grance in the

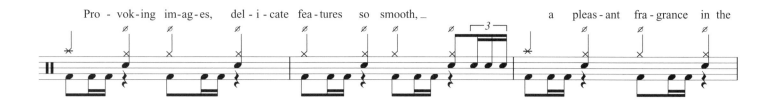

light of the moon. _ Dance with the dead in my dreams. _____

Chorus

Lis - ten to their hal -lowed screams. _____ The dead have tak - en my soul. _

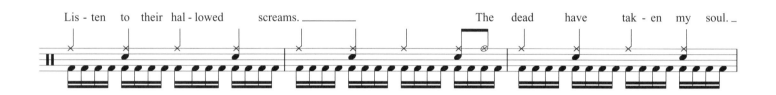

__ Temp - ta - tion's lost all con - trol. _____

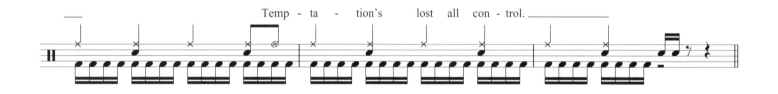

Verse
2. Sim - ple smiles _ e - lude _ psy - chot -ic eyes. _ Lose all mind _ con - trol,

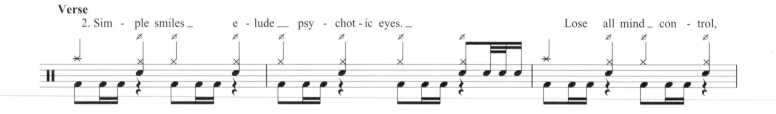

ra - t'nale de -clines. _____ Emp - ty eyes en - slave _ the cre - a - tion

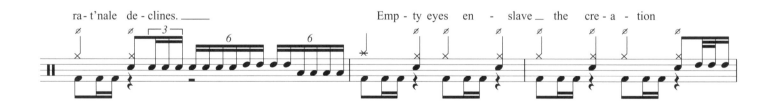

of plac - id fac - es and life - less pag - eants. _____

Bridge

In the depths ___ of a mind ___ in - sane, ___

fan - ta - sy and re - al - i - ty are ___ the same. ___

Guitar Solo

Interlude
Slightly faster ♩=110

Verse

3. Graze the skin ___ with my ___ fin - ger - tips. ___

The brush of dead, warm ___ flesh ___ pac - i - fies the means. ___

In - cised mem - bers, or - na - ments ___ on my be - ing. ___

Ad - u - lat - ing the skin ___ be - fore ___ me.

Sim - ple smiles ___ e - lude ___ psy - chot - ic eyes. ___

Lose all mind ___ con - trol, ra - tion - ale de - clines. ___

Emp - ty eyes ___ en - slave ___ the cre - a - tion

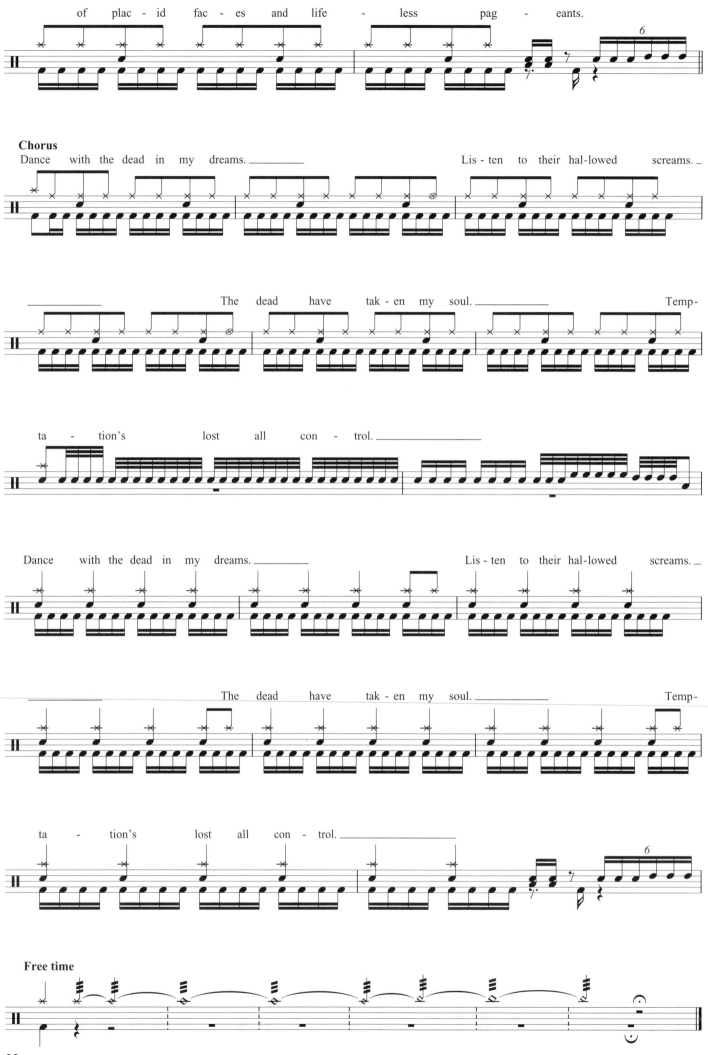

Postmortem

Words and Music by Jeff Hanneman

Verse

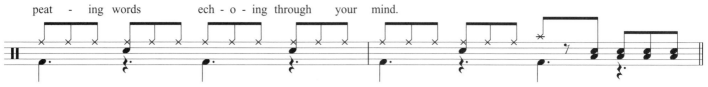

peat - ing words ech - o - ing through your mind.

Interlude

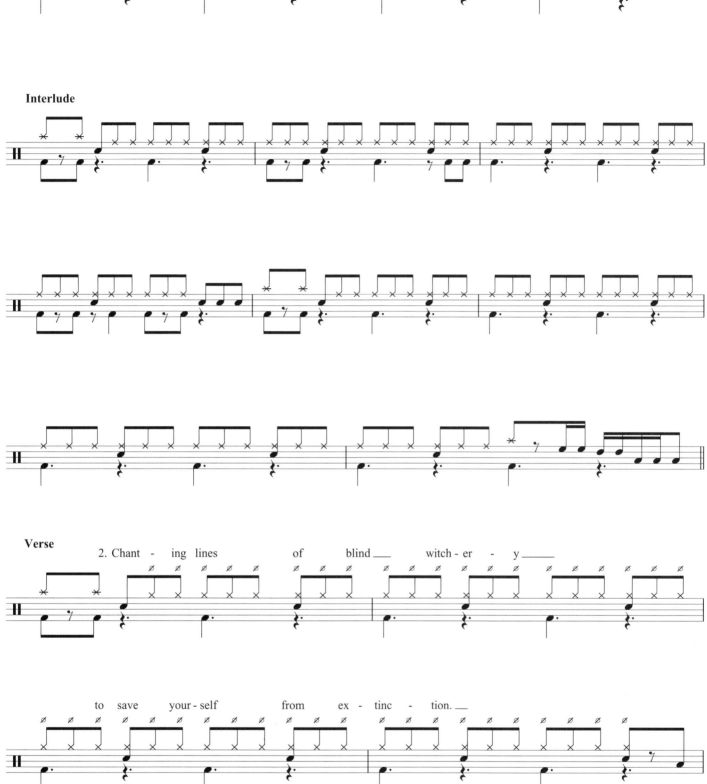

Verse

2. Chant - ing lines of blind___ witch - er - y___

to save your - self from ex - tinc - tion.___

Want - ing to die is your rea - son to live.___

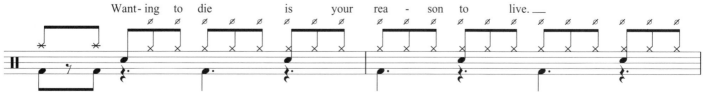

New life born from the op - pressed.

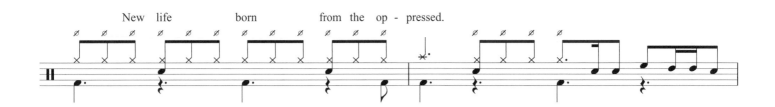

Taste your blood as it trick - les through the air. __ An -

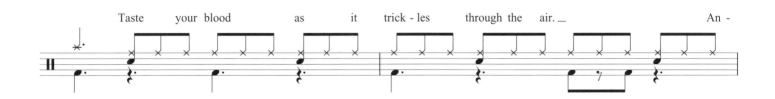

oth - er cas - u - al - ty be - yond the shad - ows you fall. __

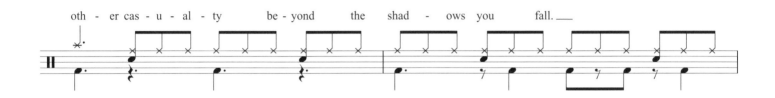

Los - ing ground, the fate you feel draws near. Fa -

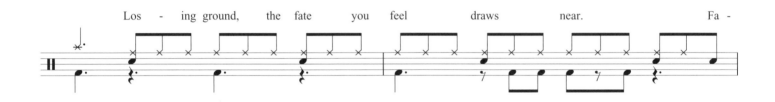

tal - i - ty, re - al - i - ty, a - wait the fi - nal call! _____

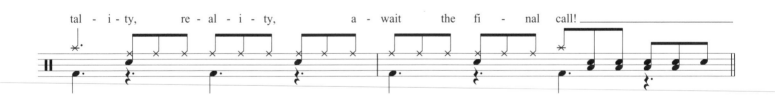

Interlude

3. My sin - ful glare at noth - ing holds

thoughts of death be - hind it. Skel - e - tons in my mind com - mence tear - ing at my san - i - ty.

Ves - sels in my brain car - ry death un - til my birth. Come and die with me for - ev - er,

Raining Blood

Words and Music by Jeff Hanneman and Kerry King

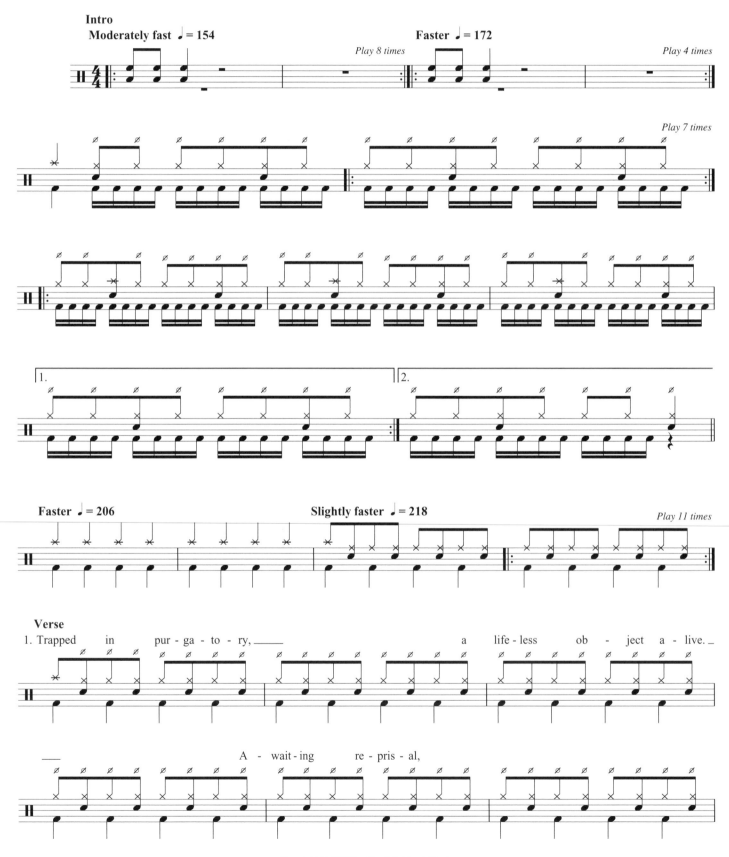

A - wait - ing the hour of re - pris - al, your time slips a -

Slightly slower ♩ = 176
way.

Play 3 times

Chorus
Rain - ing blood _____

from a lac - er - at - ed sky. Bleed - ing its hor - ror.

Cre - at - ing my struc - ture, now I shall reign in

blood.

Seasons in the Abyss

Words and Music by Jeff Hanneman and Tom Araya

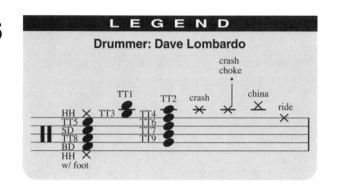

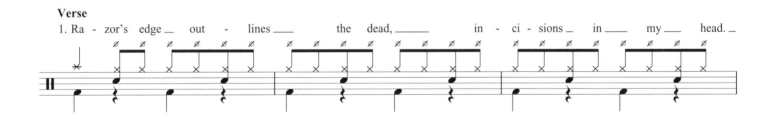

Verse

1. Ra - zor's edge___ out - lines___ the dead,___ in - ci - sions___ in___ my___ head.___

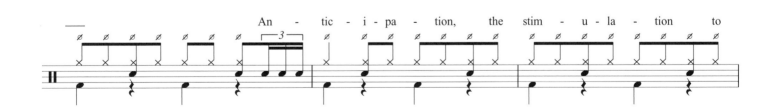

___ An - tic - i - pa - tion, the stim - u - la - tion to

kill___ the ex - hil - a - ra - tion.

Chorus

Close your eyes,_ look deep___

your thoughts   drain.   As you go   in - sane, _____   go ___ in - sane! __

Interlude

Guitar Solo

Verse

3. In - ert flesh, a blood - y tomb, a dec - o - rat - ed splat - ter bright - ens the room.

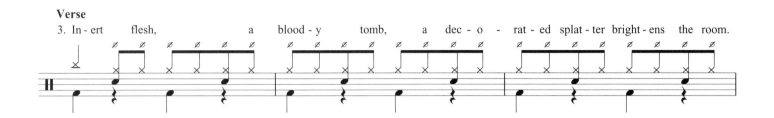

An ex - e - cu - tion, a sa - dist rit - 'al, mad

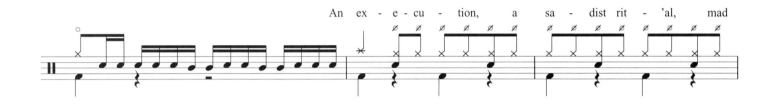

in - ter - vals of mind re - sid - 'al.

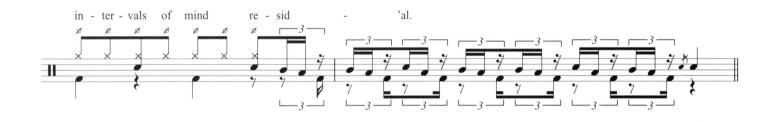

Chorus

Close your eyes, _ look deep _____ in your soul, _ step out - side your - self ___ and let ___

___ your mind go. _ Fro - zen eyes _ stare deep _____ in your mind __ as you die! _

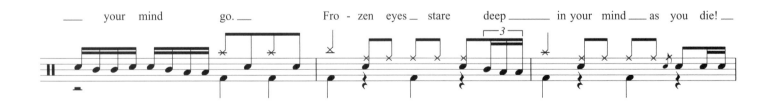

Close your eyes _ and for - get ____

your name, step out - side your - self and let your thoughts drain.

As you go in - sane, go in - sane!

Outro
Half-time ♩ = 74

Free time

South of Heaven

Words and Music by Jeff Hanneman and Tom Araya

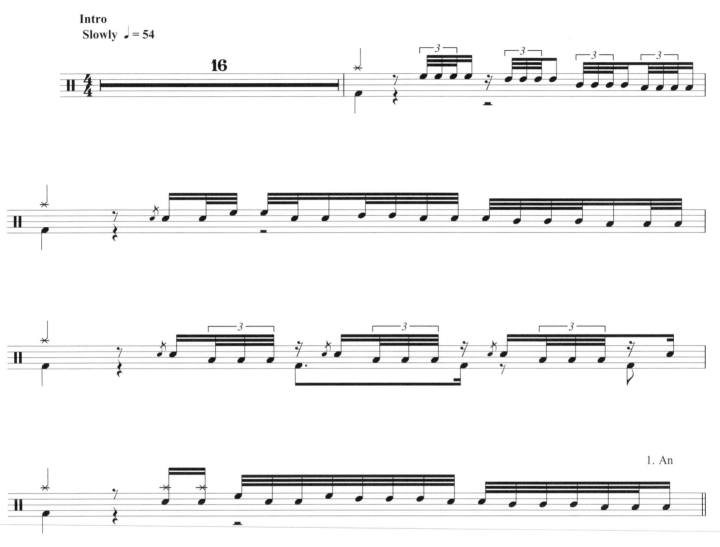

Intro
Slowly ♩ = 54

1. An

Verse
un-fore-seen fu-ture nes-tled some-where in time.   Un-sus-pect-ing vic-tims, no warn-ings, no signs.

Judge-ment day, the sec-ond com-ing ar - rives. _____

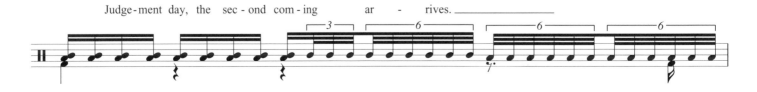

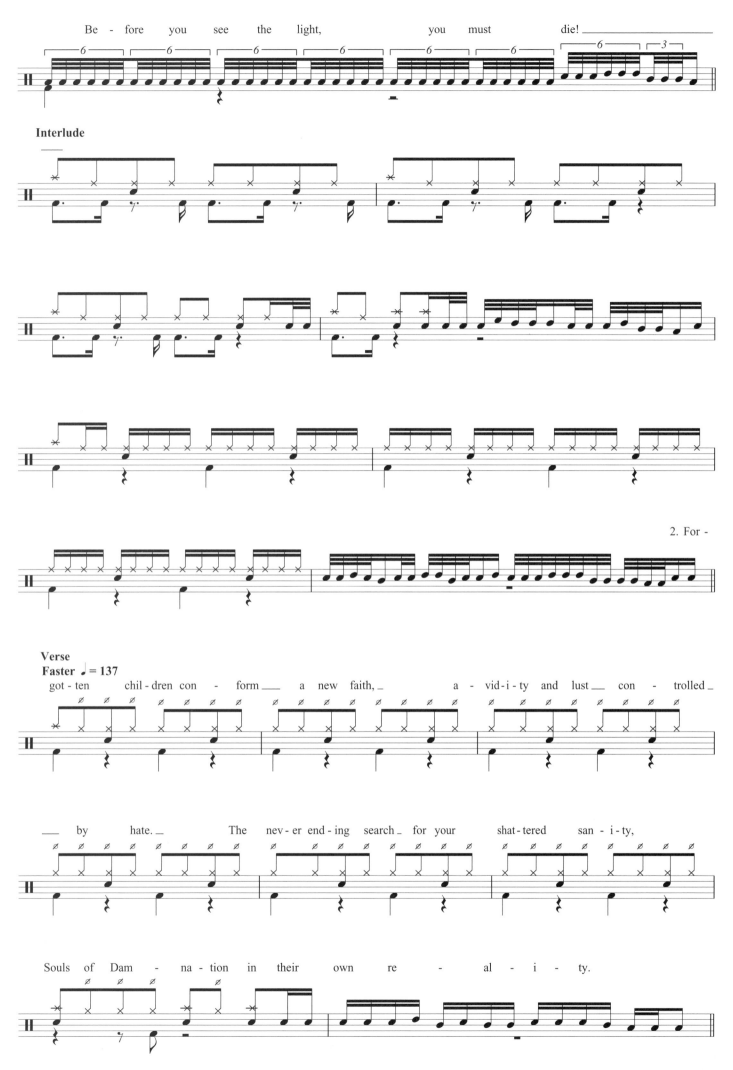

Be - fore you see the light, you must die! _____

Interlude

2. For -

Verse
Faster ♩ = 137

got - ten chil - dren con - form ____ a new faith, ____ a - vid - i - ty and lust ___ con - trolled ___

___ by hate. ___ The nev - er end - ing search _ for your shat - tered san - i - ty,

Souls of Dam - na - tion in their own re - al - i - ty.

Pre-Chorus

Cha - os   ram - pant in an age_____ of dis - trust. ____

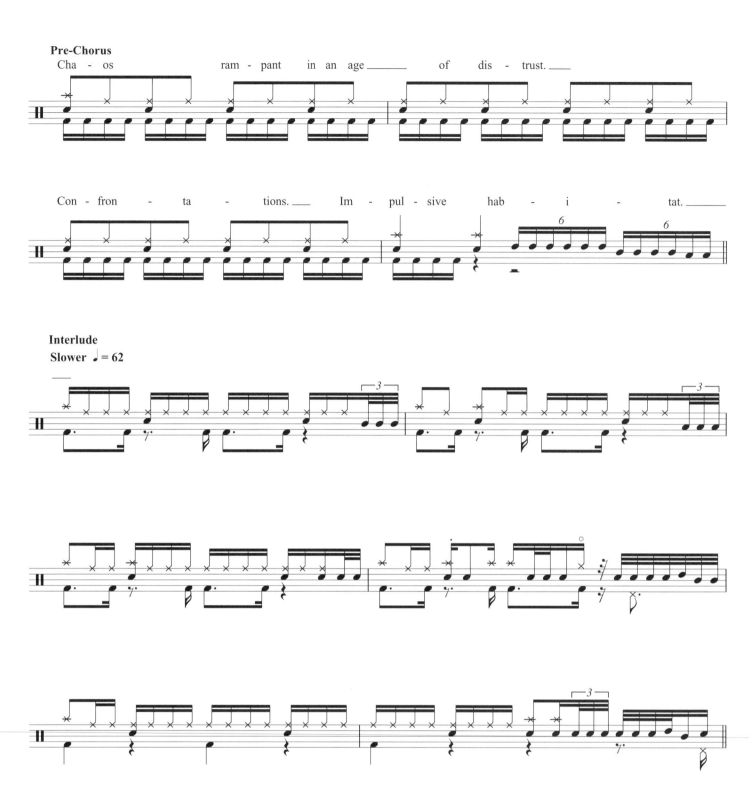

Con - fron - ta - tions. ____ Im - pul - sive hab - i - tat. _____

Interlude
Slower ♩ = 62

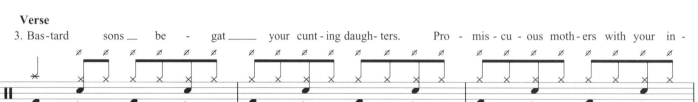

Verse

3. Bas-tard   sons__ be - gat ____ your cunt-ing daugh-ters.   Pro - mis-cu - ous moth-ers with your in -

ces - tu - ous fa - thers.   In - grate   souls__ con - demned__ for all e - ter - ni - ty.   Ob -

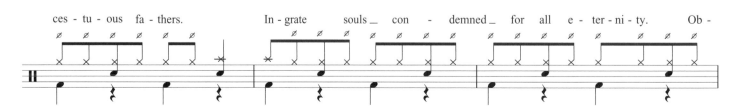

tained by im - mor - al ob - ser - vance a dom - i - neer - ing de - i - ty.

Pre-Chorus

Cha - os ram - pant in an age of dis - trust.

Con - fron - ta - tions. Im - pul - sive sab - bath.

Chorus

On and on, south of heav - en.

On and on, south of heav - en.

On and on, south of heav - en.

On and on, south of heav - en.

Guitar Solo

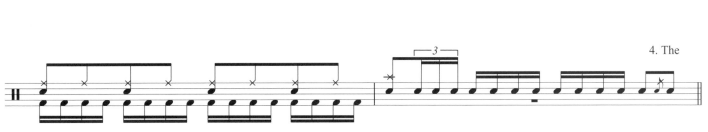

4. The

Root of all e - vil is the heart of a black _ soul. A force that has lived all e - ter -

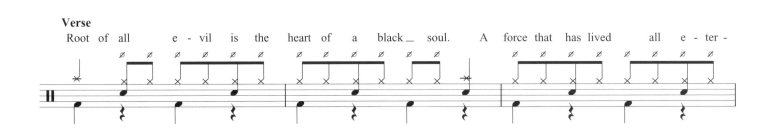

ni - ty. The nev - er end - ing search _ for a truth _ nev - er told. _ The

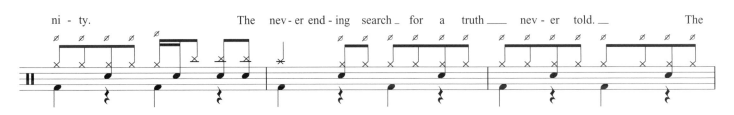

46

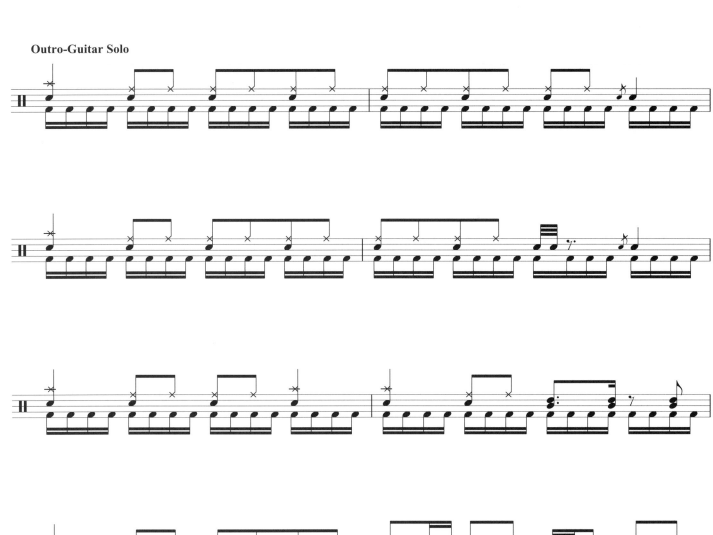